On the Road with Mitt and the Mutt

A TOUCHSTONE BOOK
Published by Simon & Schuster
New York   London   Toronto   Sydney   New Delhi

Touchstone
A Division of Simon & Schuster, Inc.
1230 Avenue of the Americas
New York, NY 10020

This book is a work of fiction. Names, characters, places, and incidents either are products of the author's imagination or are used fictitiously. Any resemblance to actual events or locales or persons, living or dead, is entirely coincidental.

Copyright © 2012 by Bruce Kluger and David Slavin

All rights reserved, including the right to reproduce this book or portions thereof in any form whatsoever. For information address Touchstone Subsidiary Rights Department, 1230 Avenue of the Americas, New York, NY 10020.

First Touchstone hardcover edition June 2012

TOUCHSTONE and colophon are registered trademarks of Simon & Schuster, Inc.

For information about special discounts for bulk purchases, please contact Simon & Schuster Special Sales at 1-866-506-1949 or business@simonandschuster.com.

The Simon & Schuster Speakers Bureau can bring authors to your live event. For more information or to book an event contact the Simon & Schuster Speakers Bureau at 1-866-248-3049 or visit our website at www.simonspeakers.com.

10 9 8 7 6 5 4 3 2 1

Library of Congress Cataloging-in-Publication data is available.
ISBN 978-1-5011-0944-7
ISBN 978-1-4516-9889-3 (ebook)

Cover photographs: Winding road © iStockphoto.com/Willard;
Romney family © Mitt Romney/MittRomney.com
Dog (and author) trainer: Brian DeFiore

For our families. And Gail Collins.

Authors' Note

The events depicted in this book are purely fictitious.
After all, who would actually tie a dog
to the roof of a car?

In the summer of 1983, a man from Massachusetts decided to take his wife and five sons—and their beloved Irish setter, Seamus—on a car trip across America. A captain of industry blessed with movie idol looks and many, many deeply held convictions, the man believed that this cross-country tour would be a wonderful way to introduce his children to the beauty and splendor of their native land. And so he gathered his family together and announced the exciting news to them in the den of their humble home.

Attention, all Romneys,
by power of attorney,
I hereby declare that we're taking a journey!

We'll travel this nation
from near to afar—
with only one pee break, then back in the car!

We'll stick to the schedule
that Mom and I planned.
You'll have an adventure—I'll bet you ten grand!

Now, Ben, you're in charge of
the maps and directions;
and, Tagg, keep me posted on local elections.

And, Josh, Matt, and Craig,
we'll need songs of good cheer
(except for that one about bottles of beer!)

And what about Seamus, our four-legged star?
I'll strap him down tight . . .

. . . to the roof of the car.

The glory of Rushmore,
it's got me to thinkin',
ol' Dad should be up there
with Teddy and Lincoln!

In fact, I've got something
those fellows were lacking,
my chiseled good looks—
and my corporate backing!

What's more, I deserve
such a notable place,
where picnicking tourists
can sit on my face!

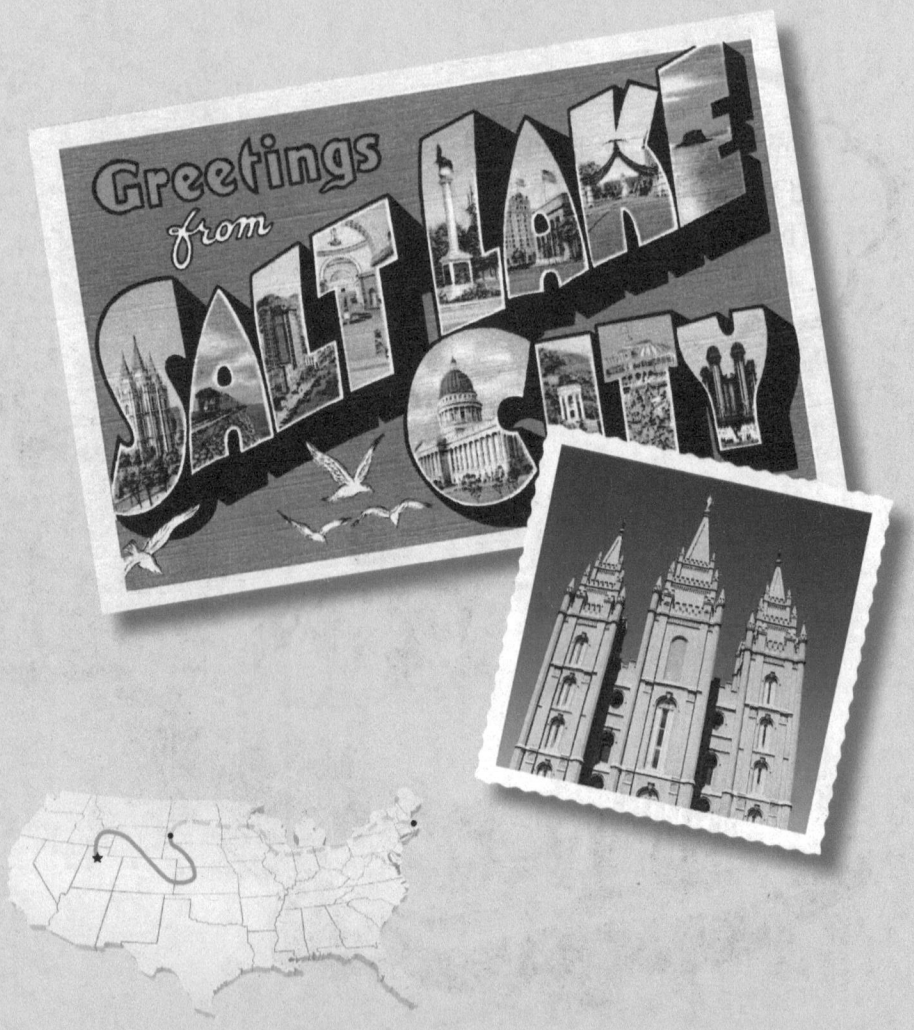

Behold, it's our temple,
our House of all Houses,
where those in our flock
count their blessings (and spouses).

We don't judge our faithful,
not even a smidgen,
for ours is a special
(though kooky) religion.

But keep it a secret
so people don't tease us—
if I run for office,
just talk about Jesus.

Now, boys, close your eyes,
for we've hit the rock bottom—
a city that's ruled
by Gomorrah and Sodom.

A village of sinners
who clamor for booty,
and bow at the altar
of Liza and Judy.

Don't mean to be prissy,
don't want to disparage—
they're free to cut hair,
but they'll never have marriage!

Look around, gang,
'cause this sight is a honey.
The Fountain of Finance!
The Mecca of Money!

Yes, Wall Street's a temple,
our nation's salvation.
And we are among
its elite congregation.

Stocks are our church,
and bonds are our steeple—
remember, my sons,
corporations are people!

Look, kids—free soup!
This is welfare in action,
as Uncle Sam cares for
our down-and-out faction.

We house them! We clothe them!
They live lives of ease,
with dignity, honor . . .
and government cheese!

Just look at their faces,
so calm and content—
they're *grateful* they're not
in the top one percent!

Feast your eyes, lads,
on these suckers and saps,
who squander their savings
on keno and craps!

We live by the standard
of Standard & Poor's—
that gambling's okay,
if the money's not yours.

But not in Sin City,
where all they enjoy
is boozing and losing
and Siegfried and Roy.

Down here at the border
they play hard to get.
But why climb a wall?
Why not charter a jet?

The problem, my children?
Our laws make no sense!
We need to build trust
(and a much bigger fence).

I know it sounds harsh
and a tad grandiose,
but unless you're my gardener,
I say, "Adios!"

Hang on to your hats, y'all,
you'll love this to bits!
We're here in the fast lane
of ponchos and grits!

These Southern-fried masses,
these dreamers deluxe—
they're livin' the high life . . .
in trailers and trucks.

But keep the doors locked
and the windows rolled tight—
I hear that the Cuban folks
come out at night.

This city's the model
for all that might ail ya',
with dozens of clinics
that won't ever fail ya'!

They're fighting disease
and they're championing health,
and all that you need
for your wellness . . . is wealth.

But I have a plan
that leaves no one behind.
(I won't tell you how
'cause I might change my mind.)

Although it's not fancy.
Or classy. Or pretty.
America's pride
is her motorin' city.

This town's an old favorite
of Grandpa's and Daddy's.
It gave us our fame
(and your mom seven Caddys).

The Japanese? Please!
Let 'em bow to their Shinto.
You haven't met God
'til you've fired up a Pinto!

The weather's no longer
so balmy or breezy,
and that's when Big Government
spoils the Big Easy.

The floodwaters rise
and the homes start to bob,
then FEMA rolls in—
does a heckuva job!

But keep on rebuilding?
You've got to be daft!
It just might be fun
to live life on a raft!

Now what have we here, boys?
Let's give it three cheers!
A home that's for rent—
every four to eight years.

It's safe from the riffraff
and everyday squalor.
(And, yes, we'll adjust
to a house that's much smaller.)

It's perfect, I tell ya',
the God's honest *troof!*
For my wife . . .
and my kids . . .

Photo Credits

All U.S. maps © Ken Chaya

Winding road: ii–iii, 10–11, 14–15 © iStockphoto.com/Willard. Romney family: iii, 9, 11, 13, 15, 17, 19, 21, 23, 25, 27, 29, 31, 33, 34, 37, 38, 41, 43, 45, 47, 49, 51, 53 © Mitt Romney/Mitt Romney.com. Dog bone: 1 © iStockphoto.com/Liliboas. Romney house: 3, courtesy of JBUK_Planet, Flickr.com. American flag: 3 © iStockphoto.com/ermingut. Dog tail: 7, 9, 13, 17, 21, 25, 29, 33, 37, 41, 45, 49, 53 © Eric Isselée from BigStockPhoto.com. Postcards: 8, 16, 24, 28, 36, 40 Tichnor Brothers. Mount Rushmore: 8, 10 © iStockphoto.com/megasquib. Postcards: 12, 20, 32, 44, 48, 52 Curt Teich and Co. Mormon temple: 12, 14 © iStockphoto.com/helt2. Base image of San Francisco: 18–19 © Michael Creasy. Composite photos of people in SF: 18–19 © dbking; Boss Tweed (2); Tim Schapker; Dejan Cabrilo, Jos van Zetten from Amsterdam, the Netherlands; theodoranian/Wikimedia Commons. Drag queen holding Mitt: 19 © Scott Griessel from BigStockPhoto.com. Rainbow balloons: 19 © iStockphoto.com/REKINC1980. Wall Street sign: 20 © iStockphoto.com/ChuckStryker. New York street with bull statue: 22–23 © Douglas Boldt, http://boldt.us. Church door: 26 © iStockphoto.com/ozgurdonmaz. Hotel sign: 27 © iStockphoto.com/Maksymowicz. Soup kitchen patrons: 26, 27 © Jeffrey Beall. Las Vegas sign: 28 © iStockphoto.com/compassandcamera. Panorama of Las Vegas: 30–31 Las Vegas City Files. Border fence: 34, 35 © Jeffrey Kaye. Fence climber 1: 35 © Tomas Castelazo/Wikimedia Commons. Fence climber 2: 35 © Guillermo Arias/Associated Press. Fence climber 3: 35 © Francisco Villa/Associated Press. Checkered flag: 36 © iStockphoto.com/Kativ. Race track: 38–39 Larry McTighe/US Airforce Photo. Boston Medical Center: 40 © Cmcnicoll/Wikimedia Commons. Emergency sign: 40 © iStockphoto.com/sshepard. Hospital hallway: 42–43 © iStockphoto.com/DanielMirer. Doctors: 42 © lisafx from PixMac.com. Big tire: 44 © James Marvin Phelps from USA, JMP Photography LLC. Car factory: 46–47 © AP Photo/Ajit Solanki. Bourbon Street: 48 © Alexey Sergeev. Flooded New Orleans: 50–51 © iStockphoto.com/joeynick. Trolley: 50 © Infrogmation/Wikimedia Commons. Floating sun: 50 Photo by Judi Bottoni. White House: 52 © iStockphoto.com/Vacclav. Police officers: 54, 55 © iStockphoto.com/rocketegg.

About the Authors

Bruce Kluger and **David Slavin** (authors) began writing and performing satire for National Public Radio's *All Things Considered* in 2002. Their cultural and political commentary has appeared in the *Los Angeles Times, The New York Times*, the *Chicago Tribune*, and other newspapers in the Los Angeles Times–Washington Post News Service. Their work has also been featured on the Huffington Post, where they are recurring bloggers, and Salon.com, which ran their acclaimed "Memo to George" series during the Bush II administration. Previous books include the satirical biography *Young Dick Cheney: Great American* and *'Twas the Night Before Christmas: 21st Century Edition*. Bruce and David live one block from each other in New York City. Both are married, and both have two daughters.

Colleen Clapp (illustrator) has created artwork for, among others, the Smithsonian, NBC News, ABC News, *The Chris Matthews Show,* and the Philadelphia Zoo. Her commissions have included public murals, magazine and book illustrations, and portraits and paintings in a variety of media. She has also exhibited her oil paintings in the Baltimore–Washington, D.C., area. Colleen lives in Frederick, Maryland, with her husband. The couple has two daughters.

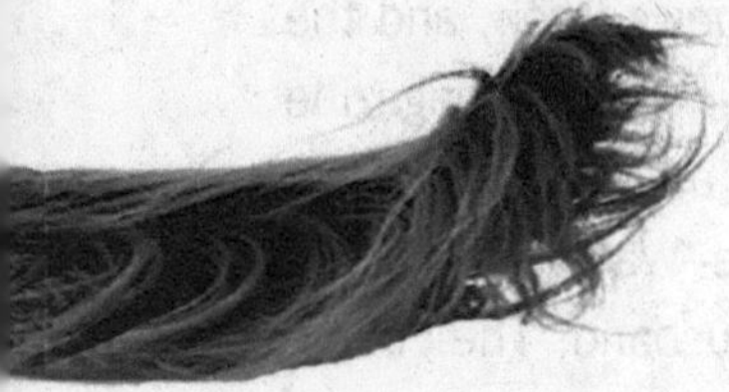

www.ingramcontent.com/pod-product-compliance
Lightning Source LLC
Chambersburg PA
CBHW011421070526
44584CB00026BA/3791